RENÉ GUENON

A Teacher for Modern Times

Julius Evola

Translated, with an Introduction,
by Guido Stucco
Department of Theology
St. Louis University

Foreword by the Julius
Evola Foundation
of Rome

HOLMES PUBLISHING GROUP

ISBN 1-55818-229-2

SECOND EDITION,

REVISED

— 2005 —

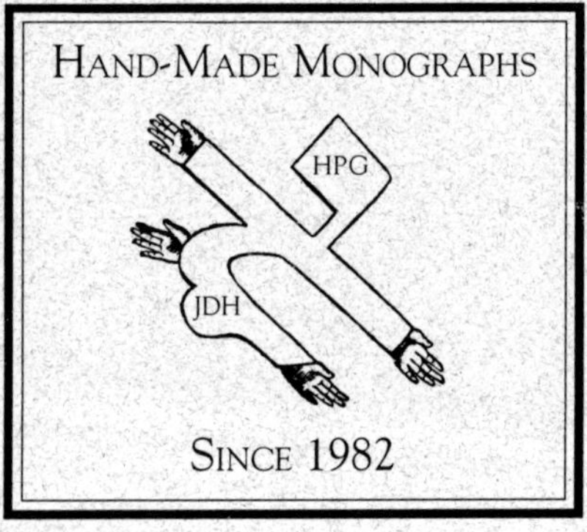

HOLMES PUBLISHING GROUP LLC
POSTAL BOX 2370
SEQUIM WA 98382 USA
JDHOLMES.COM

I WISH TO DEDICATE THIS TRANSLATION TO
MY TEACHERS OF OLD: RUDY PONT, VITTORIO G.
ROSSI, AND DON GIUSEPPE DOSSETTI.

INTRODUCTION

Who was Julius Evola? Considered by many a philosopher, others have cast him in the role of arch-reactionary. Regardless, his philosophical writings have earned him a place as one of the leading representatives of the Traditionalist school.

Like the American poet Ezra Pound before him, the term "fascist" has been accorded Evola for being among the opposition during WWII. For three decades he was shunned by the academic community which took little interest in his writings. Yet Evola has been the object of an interesting revival, acquiring a posthumous revenge of sorts. Conferences and *symposia* devoted to the analysis of his thought have "mushroomed" in the past fifteen years throughout Europe. Secondly, Evola has exercised a magical spell on many people who, having lost faith in so-called progressive ideals, have taken a sharp turn toward Tradition in their quest for something more transcendent or for something of a "higher order." These new views cannot be readily found in the wasteland of contemporary society. Thirdly, his spiritual and metaphysical ideas, far from being an appendix to his *Weltanschauung*, represent the very core and can no longer be ignored. Evola's ideas call for a critical analysis and a reasonable response from sympathizers and critics alike.

The reader of these essays will be able to find detailed information about Julius Evola's life and thought in Richard Drake's writings.[1] This introduction seeks to identify and to characterize the common themes running through these four essays:—*The Path of Enlightenment in the Mithraic Mysteries*; *Zen: The Religion of the Samurai*; *Taoism, The Magic, The Mysticism*; *Rene Guenon: A Teacher for Modern Times*. (Holmes Publishing Group, 1994.) Let us begin with the first theme.

Upon a cursory reading, it is immediately evident that Evola establishes a dichotomy between common, ordinary knowledge, and a secret knowledge which is the prerogative of a selected few. This distinction, also known to Plato, who distinguished between *doxa* and *episteme*, has been the legacy of the Mystery cults, of Mithraism, of Gnosticism, and of all initiatory chains, East or West.

The epistemological distinction between esoteric and exoteric knowledge is rooted, according to Evola, in the ontological classism which separates people, the multitudes, or the *oi polloi*, from the *aristoi*, the heroes, the kings, and the men of knowledge (priests and ascetics). One of the constants in Evola's thought, is his aversion for the empirical subject, who lives, eats, reproduces and dies; everything in his works represents a yearning for something which is more than ordinary existence, more than that condition of life which is heavily conditioned by routines, passions, cravings and superficiality, for what the Germans call *meher als leben* ("more than living"),—a sort of nostalgia for the *Hyperuranium*, for Transcendence, for "what was in the origins." Esotericism is the means to achieve the ultimate reality which all religions strive to achieve, though they call it by many names, as the late Joseph Campbell was fond of saying. During his career as a writer, Julius Evola was involved in an extensive, sophisticated study of esoteric doctrines. In these essays we find Evola celebrating the metaphysical premises and techniques of Zen and of operative Taoism; elsewhere he sang the praise of Tantrism[2] and of early Buddhism.[3] In another work, commended by Carl G. Jung, he discussed Hermeticism.[4] Scholars of various disciplines will not forgive this controversial and brilliant Italian thinker his incursions in their own fields of competence, such as history, religion, mythology, and psychology. And yet Evola succeeds in weaving a colorful and suggestive pattern, which slowly and gracefully evolves into a well articulated, monolithic *Weltanschauung*.

Another distinctive feature of these essays is Julius Evola's firm conviction in the existence of a hierarchy to which all states of being are subject. These states defy the imagination of ordinary people. In the Western religious tradition one does not easily find an articulated cosmology or for that matter a serious emphasis on the soul's experiences in its quest for God. There are the powerful exceptions represented by the writings of St. Bonaventure, St. John of the Cross, Jacob Boehme, St. Theresa of Avila, and other more obscure mystics. Since the personal God of theism is believed to have brought the universe into being, Christianity's focus, in terms of cult and speculation, has shifted from the *cosmos* to its Creator. Evola's knowledge of the Christian tradition was not equal to the erudition he displayed in other subjects. Nevertheless, he attempted to fill what he considered a vacuum in the Christian system. In the essay dedicated to Mithras he describes the states of being or the spiritual experiences of the initiate to Mithraic mystery tradition and wisdom. These Mithraic experiences are depicted as three-dimensional, heroic, cosmological and esoteric and are juxtaposed to the two-dimensional, devotional, liturgical and exoteric spiritual experiences of formal Christianity. In the essay on Zen he celebrates the hierarchical "five grades of merit," through which the initiate grows in wisdom and pursues the personal quest for enlightenment.

A third and final characteristic found in these selected essays is the rejection of theism and the polemics with Christianity, which in his essay on Guenon is merely outlined (see his comparison of the Christian and the initiatory views of immortality, found in the essay on Taoism). His penetrating critique of theism was articulated in the name of "higher" principles and not by an *a priori* hostility to religion and to the concepts of supernatural authority and revelation. What he rejected in theism was the idea of faith, of devotion, of abandonment in a higher power. To faith he opposed experience; to devotion, heroic and ascetical action; to the God of theism, who is believed to be the ultimate reality, as well as the believer's goal and eschatological hope, Evola opposed the ideal of liberation and of enlightenment (see the essay on Mithraism).

These essays are a testimony to the restless curiosity and spiritual hunger of a nonspecialist who dared to venture into the domain of scholars and of specialized disciplines, only to extract precious gems of wisdom, unburdened by technical details and *minutiae* which are the obsession of scholars and of university professors. It is my sincere hope that interest in Julius Evola and his ideas will be generated by the translation of these essays as they represent only a small portion of many untranslated works which have yet to be brought to the attention of the English speaking world.

NOTES

[1] Richard Drake, "Julius Evola and the Ideological Origins of the Radical Right in Contemporary Italy," in *Political Violence and Terror: Motifs and Motivations*, ed., Peter Merkl (Berkeley: University of California Press, 1986), 61-89; "Julius Evola, Radical Fascism and the Lateran Accords," *The Catholic Historical Review* 74 (1988): 403-19; and "The Children of the Sun," chapter in *The Revolutionary Mystique and Terrorism in Contemporary Italy* (Bloomington: Indiana University Press, 1989).
[2] Julius Evola, *The Yoga of Power*, trans. Guido Stucco (Rochester, VT: Inner Traditions, 1992).
[3] Julius Evola, *The Doctrine of the Awakening*, trans. G. Mutton (London: Luzac Co, 1951).
[4] Julius Evola, *The Hermetic Tradition*, trans. E. Rhemus (Rochester, VT: Inner Traditions, 1993).

FOREWORD

The Evola Society, Rome

Like Julius Evola, René Guenon is not a thinker in the contemporary sense of the word and he is not representative of that philosophy which, deprived of any higher reference point, has relegated mankind to that mental and cultural labyrinth in which human beings have been lost for centuries; nor can Guenon be regarded as merely another History of Religions scholar, though his knowledge on the matter is impressive and the contribution he indirectly made to the development of this discipline is invaluable. Indeed, the finding of a Guenonian influence is no more difficult than examining the work of Mircea Eliade. The influence is well veiled, yet it pervades Professor Eliade's work consistently. Similarly to Evola, Guenon shuns the expression of personal opinions or ideas. In this regard, he cannot be compared to the majority of modern intellectuals who are striving in every way to demonstrate the originality and peculiarity of their findings. These "moderns" yearn to be acknowledged as *creators* of ideas despite their unconditional adhesion to the false dogmas which are prevalent in our age. The wishful thinking of these new *theorists* produce a killing ground of the Spirit whose lethal weapons are either hopelessness or mindless conformity. For Guenon and Evola, however, there is One Supreme and Absolute Truth, which is independent from man, hidden though it is in his innermost being. This Truth has been proclaimed by the founders of all the great religions, being the source of inspiration for saints, prophets, mystics and initiates of all times and places. This Truth can be acquired by man but only when he desires to rid himself of the intrinsic limits of his individuality and to become the living Symbol and the reflected image of the Infinite. Evola indicates this is possible only through the resolute and unyielding revolt of the *I*, which breaks its chains and suppresses in itself everything which makes it merely human, and thus subject to disordered impulses and passions, an inert and acquiescing victim of its own restlessness and weakness. For Guenon, realization is the fruit of a gradual re-discovery of the Absolute, of the immobile Center which moves everything else; this re-discovery becomes reality through the intuitive faculty, which discriminates, separates and annuls everything which overlaps it in the illusory appearance of the sensible process of becoming. In Evola's view, realization is achieved through the will to overcome, or through the irresistible and sweeping *elan*, which in the course of an inner conflict, conceived as a sacrificial act, destroys every obstacle and leads back again to the Unity from which the manifested world has originated as a free act of power and of self-affirmation. In Guenon's view, realization is achieved through cognitive activity. This activity is conducted in silence and meditation and these methods are aimed at attaining the calm and super-rational vision of the one and indivisible Essence. The heroic and the contemplative asceticisms are the two great paths of approaching the Truth; they are embodied in these two figures, whose simultaneous apparition in a decaying world cannot be considered to be a casual event. Evola and Guenon are the most prominent representatives of initiatory knowledge, which, in the context of the advance of "progress" appeared to be irremediably lost for the Western world engulfed in the darkness of an arrogant and coarse materialism and a degrading and pernicious neo-spiritualism. Thanks to their testimony, we have learned of a higher view of existence, which for millennia has informed the growth and the development of civilizations, characterizing and transfiguring the lives of countless generations. In this sense, these two authors can be joined together in an indissoluble binomial, just as in the World of Tradition, Royalty and Priesthood, Strength and Wisdom, Action and Contemplation constituted the primary duality which sustains and guides the universe.

MAN, UNDER THE PRETEXT OF CONQUERING THE EARTH,
HAS LOST TOUCH WITH METAPHYSICAL REALITY

This Is The Conclusion Reached By
René Guenon After Much Study

René Guenon passed away at the age of 65 in Cairo, Egypt, where he led his life far away from the European environment. He was a teacher of our times, the defender of "integral Traditionalism," and the most outspoken of "anti-modernist" thinkers. Despite the fact that several works of Guenon's have been translated and published in Italy (I have translated into Italian what is perhaps Guenon's most comprehensible work, namely *La crise du monde moderne* [*The Crisis of the Modern World*], he has not enjoyed the same popularity and consensus of authors such as Keyserling, Ortega y Gasset, Spengler, Massis, and Jung. It is my opinion that these authors, as far as spiritual stature and sobriety of doctrine are concerned, certainly cannot stand at Guenon's side.

A contributing factor to this lack of "success" may be that Guenon always shunned any expedient aimed at winning the favor of the "intellectual" public. However, there is another more important reason why his works have not acquired a more popular affection. Ordinary readers find in the thought of authors such as the ones previously mentioned, some affinities and insights congenial to their own *Weltanschauung*, even when they criticize them and condemn them; but when these same readers are confronted by the writings of a traditionalist like Guenon, they instinctively feel alienated. Guenon does not have and doesn't wish to have any association with modern culture and mentality. He represents a different world-view; he does not speak his own mind, nor does he defend his personal viewpoints, but instead he upholds a body of principles, perspectives and values which are objective and universal, since they are the legacy of civilizations which flourished prior to the individualistic and rationalistic decline of Western civilization.

Thus, even when what is most relevant in Guenon's work (such as the critique of the modern world and the analysis of the real causes of its crisis) occasionally coincides with viewpoints which have become increasingly accepted, it still has a different scope and is always integrated with positive recommendations. Guenon shines his intellect on a body of facts, societal currents, historical events, accepted viewpoints and symbols and under this new light, there are fresh meanings, candid insights and new ways of looking at things which can be perceived by the reader who is capable of ridding himself of the influence and of the distorted knowledge upon which contemporary mentality is based.

It is impossible to present in this context a summary review of Guenon's work, not only due to its complexity, but also because *ordinary* knowledge cannot be the starting point. To classify his work is a difficult task, for what he expounds is not philosophy, or the history of religions, or sociology, or psychology, or comparative mythology, even though he ventures into all of these domains, advocating a perspective of deep and enigmatic knowledge. The cornerstone of his entire system is the notion of a transcendent reality which towers above the world of reason and of the senses, higher than mysticism, sentimentalism or philosophical speculation. The pre-modern civilizations knew the ways to establish an effective contact with such a reality. This is how, in the context of a primordial tradition, a "sacred," "non-human" and peculiar knowledge originated and maintained itself. This unique knowledge generated the lost, forgotten, and misunderstood disciplines and sciences (the so-called "traditional sciences"), as well as the only principles capable of establishing a true and unfailing authority, of generating effective hierarchies, and of conferring a higher meaning to every human activity. This was the nucleus of the "traditional civilizations." Though each civilization was different in form and essence, an identical spirit animated them.

This traditional world has been swept away—first in the West, and now, so it seems, in the East as well—by degenerative and spiritually involutional processes. With the excuse of conquering the earth, mankind has broken all effective contacts with metaphysical reality, thus causing the rise of forms typical of the "modern world", which is a pure and simple negation of Tradition. Against the confused myths and the most recent superstitions of this world, Guenon continuously emphasizes that which in the traditional world is never considered a "relic of the past," but which has a normative value, and is the standard measure for everything that can be considered "normal" in a higher sense.

The death of Guenon represented a terrible loss. His books, having been translated into various languages continue to exercise an influence on hearts and minds. Unfortunately, there is no one today who can worthily replace him or eliminate from his work the unilateral insight and dogmatism of some of his views.

RENÉ GUENON: A TEACHER OF OUR TIMES

The name of René Guenon is still little known in Italy, except by some closed groups and by those who became familiar with his ideas through a series of recent articles (written under the pseudonym *Ignitus*) which were published on the philosophical section of the bi-monthly periodical *Regime Fascista*.

This general ignorance about René Guenon is deplorable, considering that a popularization of the ideas of foreign authors such as Keyserling, Massis, Spengler and Benda is well on its way. It is true that Guenon has been boycotted in France, his native country, by occult forces, for the most part composed of antitraditionalists, who have gone as far as attempting to take his works out of circulation, by means of hidden maneuvers. It is also true that the ideas of this author, in virtue of their own nature, shun any compromise aimed at ingratiating the amateurish and general public. Guenon himself, because of his serious commitment to remain impersonal and anonymous, has systematically avoided the spotlight. However, these accidental circumstances do not alter the fact that Guenon's personality absolutely cannot be put on the same level of the above mentioned writers who are becoming increasingly popular in Italy in so far as spiritual stature, serious philosophical views, specific preparations for the field of traditional disciplines, and necessary self-knowledge are concerned.

For instance, while the reader can detect in Spengler, Massis and in Benda, not to mention the "parlor-philosopher" Keyserling, the sense of a personal theory, or an artificial viewpoint more or less dictated by the author's own passions, and thus unlikely to be "objective", this is not the case of Guenon. He never grew tired of repeating that whatever of his own personality may be found in his books should be dismissed as valueless. He even asked once, polemically, if we could really be sure that a "R. Guenon" truly existed or whether that name was just a symbol. In this ironic remark there is indeed some truth, which immediately refers to one of the main traditions, according to which a thought worthy of its salt is something super-personal. The world of principles is universal, and it is very different from everything which reflects the opinions and the personal tendencies of single individuals; this world becomes contingent when it expresses itself in a given place and at a given time through various people. I will soon expound the practical applications of such a view, which has nothing to do with common rationalism.

Guenon's activity dates back more than a decade; his books obey a well established pattern, and they have followed one another according to a logical plan. In the periodical *Vita Italiana*, I discussed the political and social aspects of Guenon's work; however, it is impossible to discuss these implications aside from the rest of his ideas. Guenon's method is rigorously deductive. His reactionary, "revolutionary" and traditionalist *Weltanschauung* is *in primis et ante omnia* a spiritual and metaphysical one. The fact that his socio-political insights and his critique of the modern world are inspired by this higher plane and are always coherent with it, confers on Guenon's views a different scope than the views of other well intentioned authors, even when his views have common traits with theirs. Thus, at this point, it is necessary to present an overall view of Guenon's works.

The initial task which Guenon set before himself was purely negative. The Western world, which is caught in the pincers of materialism, has felt a confused yearning for something "different." In this quest, it has only developed equivocal, irrational and indistinct forms of spirituality, which are a counterfeit of true spirituality and which constitute a danger as real and as serious as that posed by that materialism which they had set out to defeat. Thus, Guenon attacked with a devastating critique the "neo-spiritualist" currents which enjoyed the most success in the modern world. He did this for other reasons also. Due to the mentality of some, it is virtually impossible to talk today about anything transcendent, or about anything which is beyond the trivial conceptions of materialism, scientism, and a dead scholastic philosophy, without being accused of mysticism, theosophy or spiritualism. Unfortunately, I have had in Italy a similar experience. In order to avoid gross misunderstandings, Guenon began his work by setting the record straight.

The first target of Guenon's critique was spiritualism. His book *L'erreur spirité* (Paris, 1923) deserves to be read because it contains an unparalleled *mise au point* on the subject. It is necessary to understand that Guenon is not denying the reality of such phenomena and he is even willing to admit that there is more to them than an ordinary spiritualist would admit. Assuming the point of view of a general doctrine reflected in some aspects of Catholic tradition and in the teachings of Oriental cultures well versed in psychic phenomena, Guenon claims that such mediumistic phenomena have no real spiritual value at all and, indeed, any interest people may have in these things (very far from being a detached and objective analysis), is morbid and degenerated. Finally, the spiritualist hypothesis (according to which the acting force behind these phenomena are the disincarnate spirits of the deceased), besides being arbitrary is in itself contradictory, and the pseudo-religion which it fosters in certain environments is aberrant, to say the least. If one wants to remain within the parameters of an authentic "spirituality", it is possible to create openings, at times even broad ones, looking beyond the "normal," but only through different methods and through a quite different inner attitude. The main view advocated by Guenon, in this initial critique of the "spiritualist danger", is the need to become aware that there is a "spirituality" which far from having a supernatural character, merely constitutes a regression to pre-personal and sub-spiritual stages. This spirituality has influenced the majority of contemporary movements. These movements delude themselves when they think they are anti-materialist and anti-rationalist, and when they attempt to go "beyond" those traditional teachings which they no longer comprehend.

In relation to this, Guenon's second attack is directed against the Anglo-Indian theosophy and its occultist, humanitarian and internationalist by-products. Guenon brands collectively these currents as *theosophism* in his book, *Le theosophismé Histoire d'une pseudo-religion*, (Paris, 1921). Guenon proves to be very well informed about the private and secret dealings of the Theosophical Society, and does not hesitate to expose them, in order to show its turbid milieu. At the same time, he brings to light all those things which in *theosophism* are merely the morbid digressions of confused minds, mixed with extravagant distortions of ancient or eastern doctrines and filtered through the worst Western prejudices. Guenon's anti-spiritualism does not proceed from a hypocritical positivism (quite the contrary!). Likewise, his anti-theosophical stance originates exclusively from the need to restore to their pristine splendor certain traditional and spiritual doctrines, which *theosophism* claims for itself with disastrous results, i.e. generating harmful counterfeits and falsifications. It should be noted that all of Guenon's considerations and criticisms do not have an abstract or merely theoretical character; he is more concerned with the consequences which may arise in the social arena, in the sense of a greater confusion of the collective psyche. These consequences, which may go unnoticed by the majority of the people, but which are not any less real, are caused by a certain confusion of ideas and by the modern insane flights of the imagination. Finally, Guenon does not hide the fact that he has been given an introduction to the comprehension of what he calls "traditional reality" by the study of Oriental teachings and personal contact with them. The East today, aside from the dead compilations of "orientalists" specialized in various disciplines, evokes images of theosophy, pantheism, Gandhi, Tagore and company. According to Guenon, these images have nothing to do with all that in Hinduism is severe, virile, luminous and capable of providing the deepest insights into the problem of the crisis of our civilization and of our society; he wrote his comments on the matter in his *Introduction generale aux doctrines indoues* (Paris 1921). In this book he began to compare Western and Eastern civilizations and to criticize the modern world.

These themes are developed in a systematic and complete form in his later works: *Orient et Occident* (Paris, 1924), *La crise du monde moderne* (Paris, 1927) and *Autorité spirituelle et pouvoir temporel* (Paris, 1930). These books are more accessible to the general public and are more likely to provide the means of a higher vision into the greatest social and political problems of the modern era. In these books we find a radical criticism of Western civilization or, to be more precise, modern civilization. According to Guenon, the real opposition is not between East and West, but between modern and ancient civilization. Ancient civilization, or "traditional civilization," had followed common principles in both East and West through different forms of expression, which were relative to time, race, mentality and geographical location. The systematic denial of these universal principles, culminating in a complete anti-traditionalism, is the main characteristic of the modern world. This denial of principles stands in total opposition not only to the East, but to the ancient West at its best. For Guenon, this denial constitutes the basis of the Western world's deep and dark intellectual and social crisis, a crisis of the interior as well as the exterior.

The negative and decadent character of the modern world, according to Guenon, consists essentially in its loss of contact with the "metaphysical" reality. And in the ensuing extinction of living and dominating traditions which derive their right to be and their authority from a body of values and teachings of a "metaphysical" nature.

What does Guenon mean by "metaphysical" and by "metaphysical reality?" This is a fundamental issue, which many will fail to understand, since it refers to spiritual horizons which are virtually unknown in our times and which are unlikely to be reduced to any category employed in our modern civilization. When Guenon talks about metaphysics, he specifies that by this term he does not at all mean a "philosophy," and not even a particular branch of the discipline which calls itself "philosophy." The term "metaphysics," in Guenon's works, finds its meaning in reference to an essentially super-rational plane. Beyond what is conditioned by time and space and so subject to change and soaked in particularism and in the sensible world, there exists a world of intellectual essences. These essences do not exist as mere hypotheses or abstractions of the human mind, but as the most real of all possible realities. Man could "realize" this world, in other words, he could have a direct experience of it as certain as that mediated to him by the physical senses, only if he succeeded in elevating himself to a super-rational state, which Guenon calls of "pure intellectuality." In other words, this state could be achieved only if man proved himself capable of a transcendent use of his intellect, an intellect freed from any specifically human, psychological, affective, individualistic and even "mystical" element. Guenon employs the term "metaphysics" in relationship to a transcendent realism associated with an inner asceticism, which aims at going beyond the world, as it is conceived by religions. He who has been involved in these studies can testify that this position is not new at all. Besides, Guenon declares his utter opposition to everything which is "new" and "modern." He also complains that one of the most peculiar deviations of the contemporary mind-set consists in considering a doctrine to be important only insofar as it is "original" and "personal," rather than being true. In the doctrine of "metaphysical reality" Guenon merely wants to point out the premise which was always acknowledged by every normal and creative civilization.

From contact with the metaphysical reality, it is possible to derive a body of principles which facilitate a non-human way to analyze and to organize human affairs. These principles constitute unshakable reference points from which, by adaptation to various planes, it is possible to deduce further principles relative to a specific knowledge and to specific domains, which are always ordained in a hierarchical fashion around the same supernatural axis. This is the nature of "traditional sciences" and of the ancient civilizations, in stark contrast to the inductive, exterior, particularistic, analytical, and purely profane modern sciences, which lack authentic principles and which are unable to lead to true *knowledge*. The criticism which Guenon levels against modern scientism in all of its materialistic, pragmatist and evolutionary trajectories, is the most serious and the most radical of all the criticisms ever made.

On the other hand, once it is applied to a social and practical plane, any knowledge which tradition draws from its metaphysical premises can be translated into principles which can properly situate and organize mundane activities and bestow on them a higher meaning; these principles can also create institutional forms adequate to this purpose and prolong "life" into something which is "more than life." In this context, Guenon's deductions assume a radical character: hierarchical, aristocratic, anti-individualist, anti-social and anti-collectivist. His deductions go beyond the dualism typical of a Platonically inclined *Weltanschauung* such as Julien Benda's. According to Guenon, the spirit's fate is not to be exiled to a stratospheric heavenly region; likewise, the spirit-bearers are not destined to play in this world the part of exiles overwhelmed by sorrow, or "frozen" in a stoic detached attitude, nor that of powerless utopians. That which does not begin and does not end with the "human" element, according to Guenon, occasions precise relationships of "dignity", quality and differentiation in the various forms of life. This is how true hierarchy is born; that hierarchy was known by the great traditional social organizations. The last of its echo reverberates into the feudal and Catholic-imperial Middle ages to which Guenon naturally attributes a special meaning of value and symbol. The force which created these great historical realities did not merely derive from contingent, social and economical factors, but rather from the irresistible power from above which flows from a living contact with the metaphysical reality; this contact is eventually translated into precise relationships characterized by the primacy of spiritual authority over temporal power. For Guenon, the world of "principles" is not at all a feeble world of abstractions, but rather a world of forces whose action, despite being invisible, is not any less effective. On the contrary, these forces are even more irresistible, inexorable and fatal than that which is typical of material and simply human forces. Moreover, Guenon's considerations are truly enlightening when he attributes to these invisible and unsuspected factors, historical forms and events, the common knowledge of which is nothing but chronicle. Guenon proves to be a real master in the art of penetrating the "intelligences" which regulate history and its great spiritual laws (such as the cyclical laws) in an enigmatic way; what he has to say on the matter is not only true in and of itself, but it also and especially acts as the specification of a new method. This method plays, historically, the same role of investigating what eludes the peripheral and ordinary consciousness and what proceeds from deep and hidden causes, which psychoanalysis plays toward a dimension of the human psyche and which eludes the ordinary, two-dimensional psychology.

The same may be said about the world of *symbols* and *myths*. Guenon, who upholds a traditional viewpoint and strenuously opposes modern views even in this matter, does not see symbols and myths as arbitrary and fantastic stories, as lyrical inventions, or as naturalistic transpositions. Symbols and myths are often *sui generis* expressions of elements endowed with a metaphysical character; as such, they are susceptible of being referred to a content which is more valid than both the rationalistic and the positivistic data. This is not a detail in the context of all of Guenon's works; the richest witnesses of the traditions and of the institutions which have most fascinated Guenon, are expressed mainly in the form of symbols and myths. René Guenon analyzes them and brings out their objective and universal meaning. His comparative method generates some kind of "un-variable," namely something which is valid "always and everywhere," in the context of institutions, religions and of the genuine paths which attempt to transcend the human condition.

It is here that Guenon's hierarchical-universalistic position clearly transpires. He does not view universalism the way modern deviations do, namely as a levelling process or as uniformity. According to him, the universal is true in virtue of being a hierarchical apex, and a principle which is chronologically prior and above all possible differences; it coexists with the highest level of differentiation. It is the spiritual and unchanging unity toward which every particular reality converges and from which it derives its order, its meaning and its reason of being. The same goes for every domain, including the socio-political and religious ones. From a social point of view, Guenon finds the traditional hierarchical ideal expressed in all those political systems which follow the principle *suum cuique* ("to each his own"); in these systems, the individuals, in virtue of playing a function conforming to their nature and to their natural vocation, are gathered in classes or castes. Each caste is endowed with its own features, prerogatives and rights, and is arranged in a strict hierarchical order which best safeguards the primacy of the spiritual over the temporal. In regard to this, as an ideal model,

Guenon often refers to the hierarchical system of the old Hindu society, in which the merchant class presided over the working class and the warrior aristocracy over the merchant class. At the top of the social pyramid, there were elites which represented pure spiritual authority and pure intellectual (metaphysical) knowledge. Guenon explained that this is not a contingent or situational scheme, but a principle of order which has found expression in every place where the normal type of civilization and society existed, though through various forms which are complete in different degrees. This social order existed in the West up to the Middle Ages, during which a super-rational division of people was made, into the separate classes of commoners, third estate, nobility and clergy.

This is also the case of what constitutes the cornerstone of every great tradition or religion. In the teachings, symbols and the rituals and ceremonials of each of these great traditions, there are various expressions (differing as to place, time and other variances) of one, "primordial" tradition. This seminal term should be taken in a spiritual and metaphysical rather than a historical and chronological sense. The supreme reference point in this "primordial" tradition, is the convergence of the two powers, namely the spiritual principle and the royal principle; this convergence is indeed the heart of every social organism drawing from above the sap essential for its own life. Here one finds the peak of pure universality, and, in its external application, the principle of every *Sacrum Imperium*. In the unique work entitled *Le Roi du Monde* (Paris, 1927), Guenon attempted to demonstrate the recurrence, in various and different traditions, of the idea of the "Universal Ruler" as well as its concretization as the idea of the one source of the forces which have traditionally ordained the greatest historical cycles. Just as, beyond the variety of forms and the degree of consciousness, the various traditions may refer to one body of knowledge, which is superior and prior to them all, likewise, beyond the various centers which visibly dominate, in different degrees, the great currents of history, there should be only one center, only one function of supreme spiritual government, compared to which all the ones which we know about simply play a subordinate role. Such a notion, just as that of a "primordial tradition," should be taken in a metaphysical and super-individual sense. Whether an hypothesis, or a mysterious reality, Guenon's considerations still demonstrate that the uniform aspiration of traditional man is to go beyond what is particular and contingent, in order to integrate his tradition in a super-tradition, the existence of which is vaguely intuited, and which carries traits which are imperial and spiritual at the same time; this super-tradition is the supreme norm, precisely in virtue of its metaphysical nature. Again, this is what was symbolized by the ecumenical Middle Ages and by the ideal of Dante's view of the *Imperator*. Incidentally, Guenon was the author of a book entitled *L'esoterisme de Dante* (Paris, 1925), and of a short essay on Saint Bernard.

According to Guenon, the sense of tradition has progressively become dim, both in the East and in the modern West, in which the last expression was represented by Catholicism. It is interesting to read what Guenon has to say in order to highlight the catholic (*katholicos* in Greek means "universal") content of Catholicism, in the sense of rediscovering in teachings, rituals and symbols of the Church one of the possible expressions of the "primordial tradition." The

Reformation and Humanism brought about a complete hiatus and an acute phase of that involutional process which Guenon sees at work in history, and which he interprets according to the traditional teachings of the cyclical laws and of the "ages of the world." Following the Reformation and Humanism, the metaphysical perspective was substituted with a merely human perspective. Gradually, a decadent culture becomes established which presents certain secular and rationalistic traits. Rational faculties take the place of "pure intellectuality;" philosophical abstraction, true knowledge's; immanence, transcendence's; the individual, the universal's; movement, stability's; anti-tradition, tradition's. Simultaneously, the material and practical aspect of life becomes hypertrophied and takes over everything else. New manifestations of what is "human", of moralism, of sentimentalism, of a glorification of the Ego, of frantic fretting and running around (activism), of a tension without light (voluntarism) and of "life" in its irrational and pre-personal aspects, creep everywhere in the modern world. This takes place in the context of an absolute lack of true principles, of a social and ideological chaos, and of a contaminating mystique of becoming which sets a hurried pace for people to follow. From Europe this cancer spreads elsewhere, as a new form of barbarism; anti-tradition penetrates everywhere, "modernizing" those civilizations, which, as in the case of India, China or Islam, still preserve to a certain degree values and rules of life of a different order. Sporadic reactions to this trend are short-reaching; take the case of the neo-spiritualist deviations, which reflect in themselves the tyranny of sub-intellectual faculties and the lack of understanding of a higher reality. From a social point of view, Guenon was the first to recognize as an historical truth, not the advent of *progressivism*, but the descent of political power from the higher to the lower castes; from the spiritual elites to the warrior caste; from the warrior class to the capitalist bourgeoisie; from the latter to the masses, the ancient caste of the serfdom, e.g., socialism.

Thus Guenon ascertains that since a cycle is ending, and since it is impossible to go any "lower," one can only expect a final crisis followed by a timid recovery and by a reconstructive phase. However Guenon is not certain where and how this is to take place. The fundamental task consists in creating some *elites* in which the sense of metaphysical reality must be rekindled and which will formulate new principles necessary to establish a new order. But where is the starting point? In one of the previous traditions? As far as the West is concerned, the task would befall Catholicism. However Guenon, also because of special personal "experiences," seems to have lost that partial optimism which he had expressed in his early books. He had then conceived for Catholicism the possibility of becoming reintegrated, by arriving at the full and living knowledge of that "traditional" content which it once possessed but which is now confined to a latent stage, and by limitations of a partisan exclusivism.

Should then one turn to the East? But what East? His references to oriental doctrines, formulated in works such as *L'homme et son devenir selon le Vedanta* (Paris, 1925) and *Le symbolisme de la croix* (Paris, 1930) which were aimed at articulating a doctrine superior to both East and West, should not deceive us. The East is currently either decadent or on its way to modernization. It is about to undergo the same social and spiritual crises from which Westerners themselves are trying to escape. Embracing metaphysical elements the East still preserves in some environment or in some crystallized tradition amounts to the same as turning to similar element which the best and most ancient Western tradition still has to offer. Thus, the attempt to utilize the principle of continuity or to take impetus from any tradition seems to destined to fail; there is a requirement now for creative and heroic action.

At this point there is something to be discussed which Guenon has not yet dealt with, but that he still needs to consider, if he is to thoroughly study the possibilities of the modern world from his own point of view. There are several areas in which the West is burning with restlessness and with a feeling of revolt against the most visible forms of the modern political and intellectual disintegration. Hence, the new concept of "revolution," even on the social plane; this concept is often a synonym of an authentic counter-revolution and begins to dominate and to give a direction, in several countries, to wide sectors of the new generations. It would be interesting to determine to what degree and in what form these currents, which are radically opposed to democracy and to socialism (especially certain currents in Italy in which a synthesis of tradition and renewal is well under way), can provide the superior foundation necessary to begin the arduous task of reintegration in the sense indicated by Guenon, and thus a work endowed with a metaphysical, transcendent, ethical and social character.

An analysis of this kind would be of great utility and it would elevate Guenon's doctrines to a higher degree of practical effectiveness and closeness to those elements which virtually possess the capability of comprehension and which are beginning to acquire power. If, on the one hand, it is desirable that Guenon would begin this kind of analysis, on the other hand, the knowledge and the study of the works of this author should be recommended to the best elements and to those who are most anxious to receive an authentic spiritual orientation in our new Italy. These elements would find in Guenon's works perspectives which are far removed from any particularism and personalism. They would also discover wide horizons, powerful, pure and unconditioned ideas, and new ways and methods to recover a greatness which does not belong to the past but to what is superior to time and of a perennial actuality. I feel this to be case, since the promise of Guenon's "radical traditionalism" is the same as Mussolini's ideal of the attainment of a "permanent and universal reality," which is the necessary requirement for any person who wishes to act spiritually in the world with a "dominating human will."

EAST AND WEST — THE GIFT OF LANGUAGES

Guenon's *Man and His Becoming According to Vedanta* (London, 1945), which has recently been translated into Italian, will draw the attention of the well trained and qualified reader. Of course, it will also become the source of misunderstandings for a certain category of "third rate" critics and intellectuals who oscillate between platitudes and political and spiritual fancies. On more than one occasion I have declared without hesitation that Guenon is one of the rare spiritual teachers of the modern age, and that he is in a different "league" than authors such as Keyserling, Benda, Massis, Ropps and others of their bent. René Guenon is one of the few who really possesses principles and gives authoritative witness to Tradition. He does so in the higher, metaphysical and super-personal sense of the word and outside of any philosophical scheme or empty claim to "originality" and limitations of a confessional and proselytizing nature. As the above mentioned book has been translated, I feel the need to clear up any potential misunderstandings. This is not the place to discuss the book itself since this would take us into the technical domain. It is rather to indicate the perspective from which the book should be considered that is my aim.

Let me state immediately where the largest misunderstanding may lie. A significant part of Guenon's work consists in a thorough critique of modern civilization. This critique is very efficient and destructive, since it is void of passions and is rigorously founded on an impassioned analysis of facts, events and ideas from the point of view of the principles which are typical of every normal (i.e., traditional) civilization. The most significant work by Guenon, using this point of view, namely *La crise du monde moderne* (Paris, 1927), has recently been translated into Italian. It is only natural that those readers who have followed Guenon's critique, whether they agreed or disagreed with him, are now curious to learn about the positive counterpart, consisting of the values and doctrines to be opposed to those of the modern world. It is also natural that these readers wish to know what is this "tradition" and the "traditional spirit" so greatly emphasized by Guenon, and which he considers to be the presupposition of any genuine reconstructive work. It is possible that many people may think that Guenon's last book serves this purpose, especially because it is so heavy on doctrine; however, considering that this book concerns itself with Hindu theories, it is easy to predict what is going to happen over and over again. There will be accusations that Guenon is infatuated with the East and that he is a "theosophist" and a pantheist, attempting to distract the West from its own traditions of Catholicism and Western personalism and, thus, substituting schools of exotic doctrines in their stead. These criticisms may jeopardize the comprehension of something so important that the value thereof is difficult to overstate.

Thus, in order to prevent this from happening, it is necessary to establish the following points.

Guenon's work undoubtedly represents the best that has ever been written about Hindu metaphysics. This book should also be considered as the necessary key for those who wish to undertake in a truly serious way, outside the arbitrary reconstructions of official orientalists, philosophers and theologians, the study of the Eastern traditions in general. When he wrote this book, Guenon did not intend to limit himself to this task. Starting with the presupposition that the various traditions and religions, in what they have to offer which is truly valid and super-personal, are just different expressions of the same one universal body of knowledge, Guenon employed the theories formulated by Vedanta, in the same way in which a polyglot may use a particular language in order to express ideas frequently expressed in other idioms. Therefore, the fear of and the reactions to Guenon's employment of "oriental" references, on the part of some, are really unfounded. Guenon himself does not fail to provide multiple examples which demonstrate the concordance between the Hindu tradition and other traditions, including Western ones, about the main doctrinal points.

It is legitimate to wonder why Guenon chose Vedanta in order to give a generic example of the "traditional" way to look at the world and man and his becoming, if indeed the choice of doctrine was indifferent and if his intent was to indicate a positive and constructive counterpart to his criticism of the errors of the modern world. It can be objected that his choice was not very expedient. This objection is valid, if one means "expediency" in the most vulgar and immediate sense of the word. No doubt that if Guenon had chosen some Western teachings as the basis of his *Weltanschauung*, such as medieval Catholic and Hermetic teachings, instead of Vedanta, he would have encountered less opposition from ill-intentioned and incompetent people. However, that was not to be the case.

First of all, according to Guenon, one should not foster illusions about this: as far as mentality is concerned, the modern West is not any more distant from the East than from the ancient and traditional West. In their true essence, the teachings of the ancient West have become so alien to modern mankind as those of the "exotic" Far East. Considering the recurrent cases of misunderstanding, one should not then be deceived into hoping that if Guenon had assumed an ancient Western "foundation," he would have had a greater success.

Secondly, various factors which cannot be examined in this context, have caused the traditional teachings to appear in the main Western tradition, not in a pure and metaphysical state, but in a mostly "religious" adaptation. Therefore, to attempt to "speak" through the language of Western tradition without lowering the standards, would require a rather complex work of "integration" and of "esoteric" interpretation (Dante and St. Thomas would say "anagogical") which is not exempt from practical dangers. One of these dangers would consist in provoking an outcry from those who are called Catholic "traditionalists," and who, as a consequence of their short-sightedness and of their confusing the essential with the non-essential, would easily be inclined to believe in an attempt to falsify, "violate" and distort their own tradition. It is sufficient to look at the scope of the mental horizons of "intellectual" Catholic traditionalists, such as Papini, Manacorda, Bargellini, Comi and so on, to realize that this danger truly exists and that the "reactions" would not be any less virulent than anti-Eastern reactions.

When challenging these Catholic traditionalists, the advantage consists in being able to introduce a system which is complete in its own being, and not in need of help from other traditions, as far as a correct and metaphysical comprehension is concerned. One should not forget that Guenon always writes for an elite and that he is firmly persuaded that only by re-establishing contact with a traditional body of knowledge in an unadulterated, original and complete form, it is possible to overcome the cadaveric stiffening of forms which have exhausted their potential as well as to overcome the perversion represented by new and "modern" forms. "Religion" to him was simply not enough. Everything contained in religions is true, but only when it takes the form of symbols, personifications and points of references for faculties which are definitely not the highest, such as feelings and a reason based on theological discourse; but everything which in religious traditions is expressed in form of faith, dogma and theology, in the traditions of a metaphysical type takes on the meaning of super-rational evidence, transcendent knowledge, and of "being;" naturally, on this plane the same principles may have a different scope and lead to horizons which are very hard to attain thorough another way.

Because of this reason, Guenon has chosen the "language" proper to Vedanta, which is essentially a metaphysical tradition. This affords him the possibility of achieving truly enlightened insights into the knowledge of man, his nature and destiny, which make *tabula rasa* of so many false problems and useless constructions of profane philosophies. Here everything is restored to a grandiose dimension of incomparable certainty and of an almost Olympian transparency. Everything is pervaded by the sensation of infinity and of eternity, beyond both "pantheism" and "personalism." The first result is the destruction of the small-minded perspectives typical of the insignificant Ego. Mysterious contacts are established. One has the feeling of having come from very far away, and of proceeding toward new horizons, through multiple states of consciousness, in an adventure in which death becomes a virtually insignificant event and in which "life," the way it is usually understood, with all its fret and worries, can be compared to a journey in the night. This is not a philosophical theory: it is a primordial knowledge, which has found in Guenon a faithful and impersonal interpreter. Those who have achieved the inner "realization" (this is the only thing that matters), cannot help but smile down on those who attack either the myth of the East or of the West, because they know the terms of the true synthesis: on the one hand, the profane ignorance with its various mental and sentimental trajectories; on the other hand the bearers of true knowledge, united in a common front, even when they are not aware of it and when they give all of their energies to see the triumph of the spirit in the context of a given people and of a given civilization.

RENÉ GUENON AND THE GUENONIAN SCHOLASTICISM

René Guenon should certainly be considered as a Master of our times. His contributions to the critique of the modern world and to the comprehension of the "world of Tradition", of symbols and of metaphysical teachings, are truly invaluable. I have been myself, for more than thirty years now, one of the very first writers to make Guenon known in Italy (and even in central Europe), by means of essays, translations and quotes. I remained in a cordial epistolary relationship with him almost until the time of his death. If, on the one hand, one hopes that Guenon's thought will exercise an adequate influence, on the other hand, one should beware of a danger, namely the emerging of a Guenonian "scholasticism." This kind of "scholasticism" consists in following passively just about every view ever formulated by Guenon, with a pedantic attitude, without any true investigation or discrimination, and with a real fear to make even the slightest change in the master's formulations.

While it remains true that "originality" is definitely out of place in this domain, the influence of a teacher is truly effective not when it generates slavish and stereotypical repetitions, but when it generates the impulse for further developments, and, if necessary, for revisions, thanks to an abundance of perspectives. While an acknowledgment of what is valid and unique in Guenon's work is due, this should not prevent the observation of some of his limits, due to his "personal equation" and to his *forma mentis*. It is precisely this critical approach that leaves room for potentially fruitful work. The personal orientation of Guenon has essentially been intellectual and "sapiential." In all of his works, anything which is "existential" and practical, his personal experience, any specific directive facilitating the inner realization beyond pure doctrine, all this is almost nonexistent. Hence the danger of a Guenonian "scholasticism" (in the negative sense of the term), which can reduce everything to something which is both inoperative and abstract, despite the claims (without a proof) advanced by many followers of Guenon, of having attained a knowledge which should be "realizing" as well.

The proof that such a danger is real, is given by the orientation taken by some Guenonian cliques of "strict observance." An example is also found in Italy, by the periodical "Review of Traditional Studies," which was started last year in Turin, and which imitates the French Guenonian periodical *Etudes traditionnelles* even in its editorial contents. The translations made in it of old articles written by Guenon, along with some texts or theoretical orientations, may be helpful. However the tone of this review is a pedantic one. One can frequently notice in it an academic inclination, namely the style of speaking *ex cathedra* and *ex tripode* in a final and pedagogical tone, and with an authority which no member of the editorial staff possesses, either because of spiritual stature or because of valid works being published. In this way, that contemptible "individualism" (one shudders only at hearing phrases such as "individual realization") finds a viable outlet; what in psychoanalysis is called *Geltungstrieb* has the possibility of affirming itself, under the cover of impersonality, whenever somebody puts on the air of being a spiritual "teacher."

It is rather strange that I was the victim of such a "know-it-all" attitude in an essay featured on the fourth issue of this review. Since this essay was featured in the section called "Book Reviews," it would be natural to think that a recent book of mine had just been reviewed. That was not the case, as the book reviewed was *The Doctrine of the Awakening* (London, 1951), which was published twenty years ago, and is now out of print.[1] Considering that this review was not limited to this book of mine, but that it takes issue with various ideas upheld by me in other places, the author of the review should have considered this book in the context of my entire production. The critic mistook open doors for massive walls, and vice versa, all the while displaying a partisan and tendentious spirit.

This is not the place to set things right, since, among other things, that review does not deserve too much importance, and I would have to repeat considerations which I have already expounded several times in other places. I will therefore limit myself to say that the author of that book review is wrong in thinking that the special formulation given by Guenon to traditional teachings, on the basis of his "personal equation," is the only one possible and that it has the character of an absolute revelation, and that therefore everything which I thought I could and should have expounded in a different sense, is not as legitimate. The supremacy of contemplation ("knowledge") over action, upheld by Guenon, is disputable, since it is based on an arbitrary schematization of the two concepts, which bestows on action only negative attributes and on contemplation ("knowledge") positive ones. There is a traditional path of action as well as a path of knowledge, both being qualified to lead toward the objective of overcoming of the human condition. See for instance what Krishna said in the *Bhagavad-Gita* (Chapter 11) when he exalts the way of action by attributing to it his supreme form of manifestation.

From a practical point of view, in order to prevent the growth of any "scholasticism," action must be granted the primacy. The traditional principle of *post laborem scientia* must be upheld; the specific practical and ascetical attitude of early Buddhism is the only adequate one. Today as never before, the challenge to the primacy of spiritual authority over regal authority constitutes a particular topic relative to a greater domain, and is the cause of the problem of establishing what are the most adequate traditional forms for the West, especially when the spiritual authority is abusively and unilaterally identified with that of a Brahmanic and priestly type. This is amply contradicted by all the main traditional civilizations. In China, ancient India, Japan, Egypt, Peru, Greece, and in old Nordic stocks, at the top of the hierarchy, one always finds sacred regality, and never a king subject to a priestly class; the early Ghibelline tradition, for instance, was inspired by these aspects of the primordial Tradition.

In the initiatory domain, specific reservations must be made about the semi-bureaucratic view of initiation, as it was understood by Guenon. I am talking about the view which only takes into account the aggregation (which many times is totally inoperative) to "regular" organizations. These organizations in the modern world have either ceased to exist or are almost unreachable, or continue to exists in dead and even perverted forms (such as in Masonry, which is another area of my disagreement with Guenon).

Guenon's initial evaluation of Buddhism was plagued by an astonishing lack of understanding. This evaluation was suppressed in the English edition of *Orient et Occident* (Paris, 1924); Guenon later modified it in part, by making some concessions to a "Brahmanic" version of Buddhism, which is truly a Buddhism evirated of the specific and valid elements it possessed at its inception. These specific elements concerned an autonomous way of realization. In this realization, the action of a qualified individual who strives to attain the Unconditioned, even by means of violent efforts,[2] is the necessary counterpart of the descent of a force from above, which does not need "initiatory bureaucracies." What Guenon had to say in an unfortunate essay concerning "The Need for a Traditional Exotericism," must also be rejected, since it offers dangerous incentives and alibis to a reactionary and petty-bourgeois conformism. The pedantic representatives of Guenonian scholasticism should rather strive to reach a deeper understanding of the true meaning of the Way of the Left Hand, which is not any less traditional than the Way of Right Hand, and which has the advantage of emphasizing the transcendent dimension proper of every truly initiatory realization and aspiration.

An abstract and intellectualizing Guenonian scholasticism, typical of "research institutes," may well ignore the real meaning of the Way of the Left Hand. In our day and age, there is a deep and irreversible scission between the forms of the external life or traditional exoteric residues and any possible transcendent orientation. This gulf is deep and irreversible. Therefore, almost all of those who do not have the possibility or the vocation to completely detach themselves from the world, will find it very difficult to realize a "traditional" orientation in other terms than the ones which I have illustrated in my last book, *Cavalcare la tigre* [*Riding the Tiger*].

I cannot refer here to other distortions which my critic's review in the *Review of Traditional Studies* was guilty of. As I have said, these are things which I have discussed in books and in articles which my critic either does not know or pretends to be unaware of. Let me give you one more instance of his lack of objectivity. He makes me say that when I reviewed Buddhist ethics I recommended the use of women as objects to those who are not capable to follow the precept of chastity. Never mind reading in my *Metafisica del Sesso* [*Metaphysics of Sex* [3]] what I have said about sex and the possibilities which it affords; what I have written in the incriminating passage, provided it is properly understood, is that one should grant to a physical impulse toward sex the mere satisfaction which is also given to the need for food. In fact, any puritanical repression of this impulse could build inner tensions and intoxications which are notorious impediments to the spiritual life, or the cause of its pollution by means of "transpositions," as in the case of certain forms of Christian mysticism. I am told that the author of the review is a judge. I sincerely hope that in the court he will not demonstrate the same "objectivity" and lack of understanding which he displayed toward me throughout his criticisms.

MY CORRESPONDENCE WITH GUENON

René Guenon (1886-1951) has been considered one of the leading representatives of traditionalism, because of his systematic critique of the modern world (see *La crise du monde moderne* (Paris, 1927) and *Le regne de la quantité et les signes des temps*, (Paris, 1945) which was issued in English in 1953), and because of his masterful presentation and interpretation of sapiential and metaphysical doctrines, both Eastern and Western. Personally, I have had a cordial relationship with Guenon and pursued a correspondence which lasted to the end of his life. The following are excerpts from his letters, concerning topics of general interest, that is, not circumscribed to the esoteric and initiatory domain which was the focus of our exchange of ideas. Since the following excerpts are replies to my questions, it is necessary for me to explain the topics which they cover.

In connection to the suggestion of instituting an "Order," Guenon wrote me on July 7, 1950:
As far the institution of an Order and your project are concerned, I really do not know what to tell you. Unless it is possible to establish an authentic and regular

and 1813 it intervened effectively to complete some things and to straighten up others, at least in the measure in which it was still possible, since Masonry was reduced to nothing more than a speculative organization.... After all, when there is a regular and legitimate filiation, the decline in progress does not interrupt the initiatory chain; it merely reduces its efficacy, at least in general, since despite everything else there can be some exceptions. In regard to the anti-traditional work of Masonry which you have mentioned, some differences should be established between, say, the Anglo-Saxon and the Latin Masonry. In any event, this merely demonstrates the lack of understanding on the part of the majority of the members of both Masonic organizations; it is just a matter of fact and not of principle. What can be said is that Masonry has fallen victim to infiltrations of the modern spirit in the exoteric domain just as in the case of the Catholic Church. Of course I am not trying to persuade you, but I am merely pointing out to you that the problem is much more complex than what you are inclined to think.

A clarification is necessary in regard to the being who in the Far-Eastern tradition is called Real Man, and who is believed to realize all the possibilities of the human being. On this matter, Guenon wrote to me in a letter dated June 13, 1948)

The doctrinal problem which you are telling me about is less difficult than what it may first appear to be. Every Real Man has realized all the possibilities of the human condition, but each one has done so in a way which is typical of him alone, and which differentiates him from all other Real Men. If that was not the case, how could there be room, in our world, even for beings who have not achieved that level? At a different level, this applies also to the Transcendent Man [another Far-Eastern ideal] and to the *jivan-mukta* [the Hindu "liberated while still in this life"]; but that is the totality of the possibilities of all the states of being. As odd as it may seem, those beings who have achieved the same level, sometimes may be "indiscernible" from the outside, even in their bodily outlook; there are even those who embody a "type" which does no longer have any individual characteristic, especially in the case of those who exercise special functions. Their "type" has become identical with the function itself; this may induce people to believe that it is always the same one person to exercise this function in the course of a period of several centuries, while, in reality, this is not the case.

NOTES

[1] Julius Evola, *The Doctrine of the Awakening* Translated by E. Hutton. (London: Luzac & Co., 1951).
[2] A Gospel verse talked about a "violence" which is required to attain to the kingdom of heaven.
[3] Julius Evola, *Metaphysics of Sex* (Rochester, Vt: Inner Traditions, 1983).

traditional connection, what will come into existence will merely be an association like many others; in that event, even if this "Order" was committed to explore the esoteric domain, it could degenerate into a mere "study group," without any effective contact with that metaphysical reality which it is trying to achieve. Despite of their good intentions, I do not believe that formal associations are capable of producing serious results; thus, in my view, this project would just be a waste of time and energy. In such cases, instead of settling for some kind of travesties, I think it is preferable to do nothing at all. Obviously, it would be a different story if a connection with an authentic "initiatory chain" could be established, but like you, I do not see how that would possible.

The theory of the cycles of civilization belongs to traditional teachings (e.g., the Hindu doctrine of the four *yugas*); it has re-emerged in authors such as Vico, and, more recently, in Oswald Spengler's famous thesis of the "Decline of the West" as the end of a cycle. Guenon wrote (June 24, 1948):

The end of a cycle is certainly something difficult to comprehend, and it needs to be expounded with as much clarity as possible. It must be understood that what is taking place is, somehow, a sudden "downfall" towards a new beginning, and not a gradual re-ascent; this is so because the lowest point of the cycle eventually coincides with the highest point. After all, there cannot be closed cycles, because the universal Possibility, which is truly infinite, cannot involve a repetition. The theory of closed cycles would be the equivalent, on a macrocosmic plane, of what the theory of reincarnation is on the microcosmic plane; both theories are liable to the same criticism. Conversely, a representation in terms of open spirals, so that the beginning and the end are such only in correspondence with each other, without intermingling, cannot be equated to an evolutionary doctrine, because the cycles are portrayed to be consecutive only in a symbolic way; therefore, this does not resemble an evolutionary model. In regard to this, the widespread tendency to apply the temporal perspective to domains to which it cannot be meaningfully applied, is a source of confusion.

I had discussed with Guenon the possibility that a set of circumstances may have brought about as a consequence the paralysis which affected me toward the end of WWII. In his letter dated February 28, 1948, he wrote:

Certainly it is not impossible that "something" exploited the opportunity to act against you; what is not clear is from what quarters it came and why. In regard to what you tell me, there are things which reminded me of what happened to me in 1939. At that time, I was confined in bed for six months, unable to make the slightest move. Everybody thought this was a severe case of rheumatism, but the truth is that it was something else, and we all knew who acted as the unconscious vehicle of a maleficent influence (this was the second time something like this happened to me; the first time however, was not as bad). Some measures were taken to send this person away and to ensure that he would never come back to Egypt [where Guenon lived] again; ever since then, nothing like that has ever occurred to me again. I am telling you this so that by reflecting upon it you may be able to discern if something of this sort may have happened to you. Obviously, since so much time has elapsed, it is not possible to be absolutely sure.

Guenon had suspected that something like this had happened to another traditionalist writer, the viscount Leon de Poncins (author of the book *Le guerre occulte*). This occurrence posed the problem of sorcery, and my question to Guenon was whether the elevated spiritual stature of a given person (I was referring to Guenon himself, as well as to de Poncins) was not in itself a guarantee strong enough to fend off such obscure curses. Guenon responded:

As far as curses (*envoutements*) are concerned, there is a difference between true sorcerers, such as the ones I had to deal with, and plain "occultists;" the latter, despite their pretenses, never produce authentic results. When you suggest that these actions should not affect those who have a high spiritual stature, it is necessary to make a distinction. If you are referring to the psychological and mental domain, you are absolutely right; however things are different in the physical domain, in which anybody can be affected. After all, considering that according to a tradition some sorcerers caused the Prophet [Mohammed] himself to be sick, I do not really see who could boast of being safe from their attacks.

He also wrote:

Since you are inquiring about my age, I will tell you: I am at present 62 years old. I knew you had to be younger than me, but I did not know that the difference between our ages was so great. As far as your request for my photo is concerned, I regret not being able to honor it. The truth is that I have none, and that is so for a number of reasons. First of all, because of a matter of principle, which requires me, as you have said, to neglect everything which has a merely individualistic character. Besides, I have also realized that keeping a photograph can be dangerous; fifteen years ago I was told that a Jewish lawyer, here in Egypt, was looking everywhere for a photo of mine, declaring to be willing to pay any price for it; I have never learned what he truly wanted to do with it, but, in any event, his intentions were far from benevolent. Therefore, since one can easily lose a photo, I have come to the conclusion that it is more prudent never to take one!

A part of Guenon's letter, dated June 13, 1949, was dedicated to the problem of initiatory organizations:

What I have written in my last letter about my rejoining initiatory organizations (though I do not like at all talking about these matters, which are of no interest to anybody but me), was in reply to your sentence in your previous letter: "more often than not, outside of that sect, there have been some who had a better grasp of initiatory matters, as you have probably noticed yourself." This caused me to be concerned that you thought that, in my case, it was a matter of partaking of one of those alleged initiations lacking any regular connection whatsoever; as far as I am concerned, I repute these types of initiation to be purely imaginary. Incidentally, I have to call your attention to the fact that in my book *Apercus sur L'initiation* (Paris, 1946) I have devoted an entire chapter to explain why the word "sect" is totally out of place in instances such as the one which you have mentioned.

You are saying that in the *Apercus sur L'initiation* no mention is made of Christian-Hermetical organizations; but, on the contrary, I have mentioned them expressly in the same note you are referring to. I have not talked about them at greater length because those organizations of which I learned the existence, allow such a restricted number of people in, that they are for all practical purposes, inaccessible. I also see that you have not understood the exact sense in which I wrote about a "complex issue;" by this expression I meant an issue which includes many other elements besides those which can be known through a study conducted "from the outside;" therefore, this is exactly the opposite of what you have thought.

In the same letter Guenon talked about Meyrink, the famous author of the Golem:

There are cases in which the influence of counter-initiation is clearly visible. Among these cases we must include those in which the traditional elements are present in an intentionally "parodistic" form; this is, in particular, the case of Meyrink. Of course, this does not mean that he was clearly aware of the influence which was exercised upon him. Therefore, I am surprised to learn that you seem to respect Meyrink, also because he joined the movement founded by Bo Yin Ra, for whom you did not particularly care. On this matter, I have to make the following rectification: no doubt Bo Yin Ra is partially guilty of charlatanism and mystification, yet there is something more to him, since he was connected to a very peculiar organization, located somewhere in Turkestan, and which represented a more or less unorthodox version of Tantrism. I can affirm this for sure (and maybe I am the only one who can), since, when the future Bo Yin Ra was still called Joseph Schneider and studied painting in Paris, some members of the above mentioned organization introduced him to me one day as the only European member. Later on I even saw the portrait which Bo Yin Ra had made of his "Master," whom I recognized very well. In that occasion I realized that even his closest disciples did not know anything about it, and I, on my part, was very careful not to share with them what I knew.

Guenon and I had divergent views concerning Masonry. I acknowledged that Masonry in the beginning (such as the so-called operative Masonry) had an initiatory, and thus spiritual character; but later on, since it increasingly became politically oriented (as in the case of the so-called speculative Masonry which began with the foundation of the Great Lodge of London in 1717), it took on a very different character and historically it played an anti-traditional role; as one of the *societes de pensee*, it prepared the ground for the French Revolution. The Masonry of the Scottish Rite presents an inorganic and disorganized syncretism of degrees and of "dignities" of every kind, and for the most part it is reduced to shallow vestiges. Guenon, on the contrary, attributed to Masonry the character of a regular initiatory organization, and almost considered it to be the only one left in the West. Even though he readily admitted the state of degeneration of contemporary Masonry, because of his formalistic way of looking at things, Guenon believed that Masonry had virtually preserved its initiatory character. Besides, he limited Masonry's anti-traditionalism to some of its forms. On this matter he wrote me on June 13, 1949:

When I am talking about Masonry without adding any further specifications, I am always referring to the traditional Masonry, which exclusively includes the three degrees of Apprentice, Companion and Teacher, to which the British degrees of "Mark" and "Royal Arch," totally unknown on the "continent," may be added. In regard to the multiplicity of degrees which you are alluding to, it is evident that the connections which some have claimed to see between them, are entirely artificial. Regardless of how they became incorporated in Masonry, these spurious degrees cannot be an integral part of it. Another point on which I would like to draw your attention to is that when you claim that those lodges which did not participate in the "speculative" schism (which originated a politicized and ideological version of Masonry) still did not do anything to arrest or to rectify the consequences of this schism, it seems to me that you fail to take in consideration things which have a certain importance. I am referring to the re-establishment of the degree of Master, which had been totally ignored by Masonry in 1717, or to the action exercised by the "Great Lodge of the Elders" which continued to enjoy an independent existence until 1813. I am under the impression that you exclusively focus on what Masonry has become in Italy and in France from a certain period on, and that you have no idea of what Anglo-Saxon Masonry is all about.

In a letter dated July 20, 1949:

I think it is very difficult for us to agree on the topic of Masonry. In what you have to say on the matter, there are things which truly surprise me. First of all you make me say unconditionally (though I have specified that this was only limited to the West) that the only initiatory organizations which are still existing today are the Companionship and Masonry. You seem to ignore the existence of Oriental initiatory organizations, some of which have members, more or less numerous, even in Europe. One more thing: I have said that in the Western world there still are (besides Masonry) some organizations which are connected to Christian esotericism, and whose origins can be traced back to the Middle Ages. I have not pursued them because they are so closed to outsiders (one of them, which I know better than others, limits the number of members to twelve), that the possibility of being admitted to them is practically nil.... The date of 1717 does not mark the beginning of Masonry, but that of its decline. In order to be able to talk about the utilization of "psychic residues" (vestiges) in that period, one should suppose that operative Masonry at that point ceased to exist; however, that is not true, since Masonry still exists in several countries; in England, between 1717